REDEEMED

ELDER WILLIE SIMPSON

ISBN: 978-1-956884-22-7

Contributing Editor: All services completed by Imprint Productions, Inc.
Cover Design: All services completed by Imprint Productions, Inc.
Printed in the United States of America. Published by Imprint Productions, Inc.

First Edition 2024

Contact: info@imprintproductionsinc.com

Visit Us: www.imprintproductionsinc.com

Contents

Introduction.. 5

   Dear Readers 7

Getting Started and Early Memories 11

My Family 15

   The Children 17

Mama 21

Our Neighborhood 23

Bradshaw High School and Football 26

College.. 32

I got arrested and sentenced to prison...................................... 37

   Seeking God 40

   Kairos Prison Ministry...................................... 41

   A new release program for non-violent offenders 43

After Prison 44

  New Life Church of God in Christ and Pastor Anderson 44

  I was ordained an an Elder 46

  Lacey Springs, Alabama 46

  Pastor Anderson 47

  St. Mark Missionary Baptist Church....................................... 48

  Hotel for Returning Citizens (People Released From Prison) 52

  Prison Ministry becomes Outreach Reentry Ministry.................. 58

  Black Wall Street USA....................................... 59

  Thank You God 66

Outreach Reentry Ministry, Inc. 68

  Re-Introduction... 69

  The National Redemption Project (Three Step Approach) 75

Classes 78

Forums 79

Transitional Aftercare Programs and Facilities 80

Criminal Justice Reform / National Entrepreneurship and Job
Placement 82

Partnering with State Government and Higher Education 83

VOTE YOUR VOICE CAMPAIGN (in Partnership with Southern
Poverty Law Center'S Voter Rights Restoration Project)) 84

Project Angel Tree (for Children) 85

Formerly Incarcerated Convicted People and Families Movement
(FICPFM) 88

I Challenge You 89

My Challenge to Youth 89

My Challenge to the Church 92

My Challenge to Government 94

Introduction

Imagine being a good student and football star and squandering the opportunities that were presented. Imagine prison time.

Imagine returning from prison and going to church and not telling people that you were in jail. That's where things were in the 1980's and 90's. In my place of worship, where I was seeking help, I was made to feel shame.

Imagine it is the 1980's and 90's. Back then tattoos were not cool; today they are. If you had a tattoo, people might have looked at you as having been in prison.

In 1983 when I went to prison, there were approximately 300,000 adults in prison. Today, there are over 2.3 million people in prison.

I am proud of the work I have been doing for the past 33 years to help returning citizens.

I am devoting my life to eradicating mass incarceration. There is much to be done. We need to help people reclaim their life for the sheer humanity of it. People can change. Redemption matters. Our society needs these people to be productive citizens. Of course, we need to keep some people in prison.

I am grateful for our volunteers, paid staff, donors, partners, and the direction I received from God.

Dedication

This book is dedicated to my momma. Her name was Cora Simpson, and she was my biggest cheerleader. I am indebted to her.

Elder Willie Simpson, Jr
Muscle Shoals, Alabama
December 2023

Dear Readers

This book is about my life journey that included being raised in a good family; being a high school football star; getting a college scholarship for my education and playing football and then tossing that aside; serving time in state prison; finding God; and marriage and rearing children. Today, I am focused on helping people who have been newly released from prison to become whole and to become good citizens and wage earners.

I am the Founder and National Director of Outreach Reentry Ministry, Inc. which was created as a 501c3 nonprofit organization in 1991. I invite you to our website to learn more. www.outreachreentryministry.org. I ask you to recognize the needs that returning citizens (newly released from prison or jail) have and to help these returning citizens to become whole and be productive citizens.

Preparing People To Go Home and Reducing Recidivism

Every year, approximately 700,000 men and women are released from U.S. Prisons. That's the equivalent of about 2,000 ex-prisoners a day returning to communities across the country. Going home after being in prison is a very challenging transition for most newly released prisoners, as well as their families and communities. **Recidivism** studies show that without intervention, two-thirds of those released will return to prison within three years. Prisoners often go back to prison not because they commit a crime, but because they violate parole.

Recidivism is frequently related to medical issues and/or substance abuse. For example, a person may be diagnosed with a medical or psychiatric problem and given medication while in prison. But when released, that medical or psychiatric care is discontinued. Many resort to using alcohol or other drugs to self-medicate, thereby violating their terms of parole and eventually being rearrested.

Breaking The Cycle

To break this cycle of returning citizens returning to prison after release, we need an effective reentry "Task Force" ministry that considers the needs in all areas of the returning citizen's life.

Immediate Needs:

Here are some of the immediate needs that people have when they are released from prison:

- Safe Housing
- Trauma / Gate Fever Education
- Root-Based Therapeutics
- Mental Health
- Medical Treatment
- Employment
- Adequate Food
- Clothing & Personal Care Items
- Transportation
- A Church Home
- Emotional / Spiritual Support
- Proper Identification
- Access to a Phone
- Alcohol Treatment
- Substance Abuse Treatment
- Credit Report Adjustment, and more.

Ongoing Needs:

Here are some of the ongoing needs:

- Life-Skill Training & Preparation
- Employment
- Income To Cover Ongoing Expenses
- Education and/or Vocational Training
- Spiritual Guidance / Support / Mentoring
- Mental Health
- Substance Abuse Treatment
- Professional Services Counseling
- Family / Marital Counseling
- Aftercare

Thank you.

Getting Started and Early Memories

I was born on September the 12th, 1954 in a little city called Florence, Alabama. I was the middle child and the only boy in the family. My mom was Cora Simpson, and my dad was Willie Simpson, Sr., so my name was Willie Simpson, Jr.

I remember growing up during segregation in the South. It was an era with black and white bathrooms (colored restrooms). When I went into stores, I had to go in the back door because I was not allowed to enter using the front door. When we went to the theater, we had to sit upstairs; they did not allow us to sit downstairs in the main area.

I remember an exception to this, with a little bookstore in downtown Florence called Anderson's Book Store. We could enter the bookstore through the front door. Mrs. Anderson, the white lady who owned the store, she wasn't into segregation, that kind of stuff. She was very special, a very sweet lady. When we went into the bookstore we went to our little corner and sat down and read. I have great memories of that. Looking back, I think that's where I gained an appreciation for books and learning.

Mrs. Anderson was very nice to us. She was elderly and she might have been a grandmother. She had a very strong, positive impact on me. The people who owned Anderson's Book Store now own Books-A-Million, Inc. which has more than 250 locations in 32 states. One of the sons was named Charles and we went to the same school. Today, Charles is head of Books A Million and he lives in Indian Springs, outside of Florence. Perhaps one of the reasons the family was able to grow the business from that small downtown location is because they are good people.

The world is different now than it was then.

Back then, we didn't have much. We had no car and no television. When we got a phone, it was a rotary phone, and we used a party line. A party line is a shared line; we did not have individual cell phones back then. When I was growing up, I had to remember a person phone number to make the call. My elementary school was named W.C. Handy Elementary School. It was segregated, it was all black. We were not integrated. Today, the school is a daycare center.

I could go to certain sides of town. I came up in the Martin Luther King, Jr. era. When Martin Luther King Jr. was on television giving a speech, I would go to other homes to watch because we did not have a television. Growing up in a neighborhood with a lot of children, we would go from house to house so that we could watch TV.

I think of my family as a real-life family. We were a pretty tight family and growing up we spent a lot of time with each other. I have fond memories of Thanksgiving and Christmas. For several weeks before Christmas, my mother and grandmother would start cooking. As we would say, they cooked up a storm. Each of the kids had a specific cake or pie that we wanted. My favorite was caramel cake cream, a big three-layer cake. We always had one of the delicious cakes.

My grandmother and mother would make these desserts for us kids. The house would smell so great with cakes and pies cooking and turnip greens and chitlins on the stove. It seemed like all the moms and grandmothers cooked like my mother and grandmother. The neighborhood was fun we would go from house to house and eat. They would start cooking about a week before Thanksgiving and about a week before Christmas. The holidays were always a big family get together, a big event, a very special time. In the neighborhood, the kids would go to each other's house. The families would be the same way, with cakes, pies, and great smells. It was a tradition.

I entered high school in 1971. While growing up in that era, I developed a great determination to be all that I could be. I wanted to be everything I could be when I was a child. As an athlete, I wanted to be the best on the field. I wanted to be smart. I wanted to study when I went to high school. I might have been one of the 10 top students in my high school. My best subject was algebra; it just came to me. I loved school. I loved school sports.

I was never in a gang. I was an independent person. I grew up on a nice side of town in a family home. Back then, we were friendly to each other. When walking down the street, we would say hi to each other and especially to older people. I was a likable guy. People knew that I was not a bully. Even from my early years playing sports I was a team player.

Back then, we didn't stay in the house much because we were always outside, playing basketball, football, and going to the ice-skating rink. Back then, we didn't have video games and stuff like that. I usually dealt with people older than me, guys a little older than me. For the people my age, I was like, a big brother to them. They always looked up to me.

My Family

My parents, Cora and Willie Sr. were together. They had seven kids, and I was the middle child. I was raised by both parents. My dad was an easy-going kind of guy, real laid back and quiet. He worked all the time and was the real breadwinner, but my mom also worked. She worked as much as he did, but her wages were pretty low. Both were making sure the bills got paid. The family was stable.

My mom was something else. She was my biggest cheerleader. I have memories of her running around in church to celebrate me and what I was speaking about in the Spirit of God.

I grew up in a bootleggers house. My grandmother's name was Henrietta and she lived with us and was a bootlegger. I have strong memories of hanging out with my grandmother. Looking back, I realize I was just as tight with my grandmother as I was with my mother. I've never been a drinker, perhaps the reason is that I used to see people drink and get drunk. It was awful and I didn't want to be like that. Grandma was like my mom; they both were gung-ho about me and happy that I was a boy. As I was growing up, I was the only boy child. So, it was me and my dad in a house of ladies and girls. I got a lot of attention because I was the boy child. My grandma and mom were very protective of me. My nickname growing up was Cisco.

I was in the middle of two eras, moving from segregation to integration. My older sisters went to segregated schools. My younger sisters went to white schools.

The names of the kids were, from oldest to youngest: Jenn, Deloris, Mattie Lou, Willie, Jr. (me), and the triplets Reginald, Renea, and Regina. As the middle child, I thought of my siblings as the older ones and the younger ones. Reginald died when he was very young. I remember getting a lot of encouragement from my sisters. I remember feeling that it was a blessing to be growing up at that time. Renea and Regina were always little girls to me because they were much younger than me. As their big brother, I think they looked up to me. When I was incarcerated, they stayed in contact with me with their visits and letters.

The family was stable, and we were all smart. All of the kids went to school. I was positively influenced. My older sisters treated me good, and my younger sisters were always like my baby sisters. My sisters weren't into sports, but they would come and watch me play.

I felt pride for growing up in Florence.

The Children

I am blessed that I had fantastic relationships with my siblings.

My sister Jenn

I was an infant when Jenn died, so I have no direct memories of her. The family spoke of her as being smart in school and being a lovable young lady.

My sister Deloris

Deloris was my oldest sister, about fifteen years older than me. She was like my mother. She kind of raised the kids because my mom worked, and she was so much older. She was like the mama when mama was not home. I had a good relationship with her.

Deloris's life took her to Nashville, and she raised four children. She moved to Nashville and had one girl (Corita) and three boys (Douglas, Derek, and Dion) who were about ten years younger than me. Tennessee State University is in Nashville so when I went there for college, I got to know my niece and nephews. The boys were like my little brothers and that was fun because I never had any brothers. It was a terrific time for me with my sister's family in Nashville. I have good memories and am grateful for that time together. It was a terrific time; I could go over there to visit.

Deloris passed away recently and had been sick for some time. She had not been home for four or five years when she visited my sister Renea who was living in the family home. Deloris stayed at the family home and was there when she died in my mother's bed. She just drifted off and died.

My sister Mattie Lou

Mattie Lou is the next sibling. Of all the siblings, I was the closest to her because she was just 1½ years older than me. We were close and I had a great relationship with her. She looked out for me even when I was doing time in prison. I could definitely count on her. She was a nurse and had a great job. She really looked out for me. I found out later that my mom had asked her to look out for me when I went to prison. I remember that on many occasions, she would sit me down and talk about how gifted I was. When I got in trouble for little things and then when I was in prison, she was very concerned about me. Always, always, always.

There was a street in our city called Mattielou Street. When we were kids, our mom would take us there a lot to look at the sign. She was the first in the family to finish college and she became a nurse. She was really in my corner.

Willie, Jr.

I was the son, in the middle. While growing up, I thought of me as having two older sisters (because I did not remember Jenn) and two younger sisters.

Triplets

The triplets were born after me. It was Reginald, Renea, and Regina. I was about ten years older than them, and I felt a lot of excitement when they were born.

My mom was the first lady to have triplets in the hospital she was in. My mother's nurse was Mary Hughes, who was the mother of Jimmy Hughes who was a rhythm and blues singer and songwriter with a great reputation in our city and nationally. That was a big deal. He was very successful in the mid-1960s. His hit song "Steal Away" was important in the early development of the Muscle Shoals music industry.

My brother Reginald

Reginald was sick when he was born. Although I spent time with him, I don't have many memories because he passed away at such a young age. I was about five years old when he died of leukemia at age one. After my brother passed away, mom became over-protective of me.

My sister Renea

Renea became a writer and is a published author of more than twenty books. She lives in the home house we grew up in. She is an impressive poet and a remarkable storyteller. A recent book is *"Soul Sister Survival: Backroads."*

My sister Regina

Regina began working right out of high school and she also got married. She was into the world. She married Walter and they have been married for a long time. I knew Walter while growing up. I have good memories of my family. I always thought of Renea and Regina as being my little sisters and being cool.

Mama

Mama was a true inspiration to me. She was my personal cheerleader throughout my life of ups, and downs, and ups again. I always knew she was proud of me. She showed me her love. She was always a cheerleader for me. In fact, when I went to prison and got out of prison, she was my biggest cheerleader. She knew me. I had a special relationship with her.

Mama worked hard while I was growing up. She was a cook and worked in a restaurant. She came to hear me preach. She loved to hear me preach the gospel and I knew from watching her and speaking with her later that she was always moved by what I said.

When I got out of prison, and I was changing my life, I wanted to do right by how my mother saw me. She was able to see me start out as a young minister preaching the gospel after I was released from prison. She was able to see that I had changed my life. She was so proud of me when I was at All Saints University in Memphis, Tennessee, at the Church of God in Christ, where I became an ordained elder. She was very excited about that. I felt good to make her proud.

When she left this earth, I was devastated. She was always in my corner, always. What I always remember is that she knew that I had changed my life. I felt motivation from mama to go as far as I can go, to go as high as I can go, to be all that I can be.

She was always a very positive person who knew about removing obstacles that hinder you from advancing in your goals. Her dealing with obstacles was a model for me in dealing with obstacles. I am well-organized and I like to do all the i's and cross all the t's. I learned that from my mother. When she'd wash our clothes, she would put them in order. When we ate, the silverware and spoons were in order at the table.

Even today, in our transitional facilities and when the guys get out of prison and come to the transitional facilities, they call me a neat freak because I keep everything in order, the silverware and spoons, the food items in the refrigerator, and my apartment. I'm just like that.

Thank you, Mama, for inspiring me. You always had a way of lifting me up.

Our Neighborhood

Our family grew up on the east side. Because I grew up there and had a good reputation in sports, I was considered a pretty good guy from a nice family and people were kind to me. Although we had black and white, it was mostly white. The east side was considered the good side of town. We had the chief of police and his son who played ball with us. A lot of people in the neighborhood had major positions in the city and children in my high school were like John Anderson, son of the Anderson family that owned the now famous bookstore.

It was a close-knit, cool neighborhood. We did not have computers. We were outside kids, shooting baskets and playing football. I was always going, always playing sports and that was not unlike a lot of the guys. We played football with kids in the neighborhood and from the street a few of blocks over.

My friend Walter, who married my sister after high school, lived on the Black side of town, the west side. It was known as the hood. Walter introduced me to a lot of stuff. The west side is where all the clubs were and all that kind of fun. There was nightlife and a fast-living style. I got in trouble because I liked the nightlife. I hung out on the west side of town. I'd play ball there and go to the clubs on the weekends. Sometimes I just was not around our home because I was outside and a lot of time I was not in our neighborhood because I had gone to the westside neighborhood.

The west side wasn't wet. In other words, they didn't have liquor stores. But people could buy liquor in a bootleg club or buy it from someone on the street. The west side felt like another world from my neighborhood. There were bootleggers in the black neighborhood. I got exposed to gambling.

W.C. Handy Elementary School

I walked to W.C. Handy Elementary School. It was a segregated school with all black students. It was close to our home, just a 15-minute walk. William Christopher Handy was born in my hometown of Florence and he became known as the Father of the Blues. Every year there's a big festival in Muscle Shoals to celebrate him, the W.C. Handy Music Festival. It is a weeklong celebration of the musical heritage, including the cities of Florence, Sheffield, Tuscumbia, and Muscle Shoals. Locally, it is called Handy Week.

As a kid, I know the segregation had a negative impact on me. Sometimes we felt devastated by it. I was a mischievous kid.

Then I finished sixth grade…

Appleby Junior High

They integrated the schools when I was in seventh grade, about 1968. When I came out of the sixth grade and went into the seventh grade, Appleby Junior High was still segregated, and they integrated it. During that period, we had Freedom of Choice. Freedom of Choice was a free transfer plan and it aimed at the integration of schools in states that had a segregated educational system. We had a couple of white schools I could go to either one.

Bradshaw High School and Football

I graduated from high school in 1975 and I have many memories. My high school years were awesome, and it was a definitely worthwhile experience for me. I liked school, was a good student, played sports, and had friends. I missed very few days. I loved all my courses and math, history, and social studies were the best. I played sports and had friends. In math, we did it all by hand, using our mind. We had no computers and no calculators.

The school was close to our house, and I usually walked. We had football practice early in the morning and in the evening. Kids did ride buses to and from school, but I usually walked. I remember school getting out at three o'clock and many of the students went home on the bus and I stayed because I had football practice.

When I was at Bradshaw High School, it was transitioning from being all black to being integrated. I remember that the high school felt like it was in total chaos. I remember having black teachers and liking that.

I had a job in the 11th and 12th grades

I was lucky. The city had a youth program, and I got a summer job. In the beginning, I worked at the city's recreation center, but then I had an opportunity to work at a local sporting goods store, which was a very good experience for me. Having a job with responsibilities and learning from others, which was pretty cool. Of course, it felt really good to earn my own money.

As a Kid Growing Up

As a kid growing up, I was always outside being active, just playing sports in the neighborhood with the other kids. Back then, we had little organized sports, except in high school. I never had video games to get into and rob me of that outdoor life experience.

I was a mischievous kid and that escalated to me getting into trouble, with minor incidences and charges with the police. I first became involved with the law in my sophomore year when I was about 16 years old.

In the early years of my involvement with the law, there were several factors that helped me out. One, I grew up in a good neighborhood, the close-knit neighborhood on the east side. Growing up on the east side, I was considered a pretty good guy from a nice family. As I have written, the east side was mostly white, but it was integrated. Growing up in that neighborhood affected my reputation. I was treated with a certain amount of leniency, certainly more than if I had grown up on the west side which was the black neighborhood, in the hood. As I look back, if I had been living in the black neighborhood, I would have been treated much less favorably, to put it mildly.

Another factor that helped me out with the law was that I had a great football reputation. This caused people in authority to treat me differently. I was looked at as a cool dude because I was a good football player.

Looking back, I think I might have gone a long way in football, but I was with the wrong type of people.

I often get asked, "What got you started on the wrong path?"

In high school, I remember an incident when I was smoking a joint with a classmate in the high school hallway. The coach saw me with this guy. The other guy got suspended from school and he moved to another city to finish high school. I got to stay, with only a mild discipline. I was needed on the team.

The answer is that I was adventuresome, and I began hanging out with the wrong people. I fell for that trap of my "friends" double-dog daring me to do something. I fell for that, and I would take the dare. Most of the time I got a spanking on my wrist because of my reputation.

Football

I was a gifted athlete in high school. I have memories that some of the guys in our school were just as good as I was, or even better, but they did not go out for the team. It must have been my season; it must have been my time.

In the seventh grade, I weighed about 175. In high school, I was about 5' 10" and weighed 232. Back then, I was big and thick, just like my daddy. As young kids on the football team, we were very competitive. Although the school seemed like it was in total chaos, it did not seem that way on the football team.

On the football field, we came together because we had black coaches and white coaches, and we had black players and white players. We had friction, but we had a will to win so everybody seemed to put their differences aside.

However, things were entirely different in the classrooms and in our city. It was definitely rough going through racial integration in our school and city. But on the field, it was different.

I ran track and played basketball on the high school team, but my sport was football. I was really gifted at football. During football practice and in games, it felt like the lights would come on inside of me. I felt so energized and alive.

The big football play that created my reputation

Even as a freshman, I knew I was a pretty good football player. Our team had some seniors who were white, and I knew they were going to be the starters. On about the third game of the season, our very talented tailback named Danny Lazenby broke his leg while running a play.

The coach called on me to take his place. I went into the game and the coach wanted me to run a "a tailback at six" play. I will never forget it. I ran onto the field and told the quarterback the play. The quarterback pitched me the ball and I ran a sweep clean. I looked back on the other side and there was nobody on the other side. So, I pivoted and went for the sideline and sped down the field for a touchdown.

It was amazing. I could hear people on the sidelines and in the stands yelling, *"He's going for a touchdown."*

It's my first play in a game when I was in high school. Most of the guys on the team were white. It was amazing. It was a 60-yard run. People were jumping up and down and yelling and screaming. Man, I scored that touchdown. I scored that touchdown. My life changed after that touchdown.

Talk about a WOW moment. From that point forward, my reputation was born.

Summer of 1973 – before my junior year

My high school teammate, Ronnie Swoopes, and I received offers to attend Tennessee State University in Nashville, Tennessee on a football scholarship. I got invited to visit the campus during the summer. It was quite a thrill for me and my family. Nashville was about 130 miles from home.

Our agent's name was Rudolph Nails. He took us to Tennessee State University and after getting back home, I signed my scholarship. My friend Ronnie decided to go to the University of Georgia to play defense. In 1973 before my junior year even started, I knew I was going to college to play football.

Going into a decline – I was my own worst enemy.

Things changed for me in my junior year and in fact my life went into a decline. I had already signed a college scholarship and I started skipping football practice. I didn't see it then, but I was going downhill. I was doing good in school, and I had strong years in football, but in my senior year I lost my spot as a running back on the team. I started missing practice, I started hanging out with other kids and just stopped being the kid I used to be. They had someone else take the position instead of me.

They didn't keep me on the bench because I still had a lot of talent to run and score touchdowns. Now, instead of being the tailback, they put me in as a flanker to catch the ball. We went from being a running team to being a passing team and I was able to score after catching the ball. The coach even had me kicking the ball. I was able to overcome my mistakes of missing practice and still be a star on the football field.

College

After high school graduation, I eagerly anticipated starting college at Tennessee State University in Nashville. Excitement filled me as I looked forward to both learning and playing football. The proximity of my sister Deloris and her family, just 130 miles away, made the transition even more enjoyable.

I began college in 1975 on a football scholarship, joining fellow freshmen two weeks ahead of upperclassmen. Housing, classes, and football activities were all on campus, providing a centralized experience. Despite this, I often ventured into the city to visit my sister and explore Nashville's nightlife.

Studying business administration, I maintained my academic excellence from high school. However, my passion for learning was occasionally hindered by my inclination towards the vibrant Nashville nightlife. My college football journey at Tennessee State University spanned two seasons (1975-77), during which I played as a defensive back, a shift from my high school offensive back star status.

The transition to college football was a stark contrast to high school fame, with increased competition and a change in position. Despite my initial struggles, I formed a bond with a fellow Alabamian, William Beck, who played defensive end. Unfortunately, my penchant for late-night outings affected both my academic and athletic performance.

Though I managed to balance studies and football practices, the late nights took a toll, affecting my on-field performance. Away games, traveling by bus to various cities and colleges, provided exciting experiences. Building camaraderie with teammates in Watson Dormitory was a highlight, despite the challenges of studying in a dorm filled with athletes.

I joined a fraternity, expanding my social circle beyond teammates. The coaching staff, led by the legendary Coach John Merritt, shaped my college football experience. Coach Joe Gilliam, my immediate coach, took over after Coach Merritt's passing. Despite having good memories with teammates, my college journey was cut short after two years due to legal troubles, preventing me from graduating. Life took an unexpected turn, and I wish I had completed my college education.

I had family in Nashville

My sister was in Nashville with her husband Douglas and their children. The kids were all young when I was there. Her daughter was Corita and they had three boys, Douglas, Derek, and Dion. The boys were like my little brothers and that was fun because I never had any brothers growing up. They lived in an apartment complex, and it was nice to have family to visit and to be away from campus or the clubs and venues. I have special memories of that time with them.

I enjoyed the night life

While I was hanging out in Nashville and enjoying the nightlife, I was meeting certain kinds of people, and one thing would lead to another thing. I stayed out late, spending time in music venues and strip clubs. I didn't stay out all night, but I was out there doing a lot.

At the time, I didn't have much money and I did not have a job. I needed money to go out. I did not have a car. Being on the football team, well, there were a lot of ladies involved with us and they usually had a car. When they wanted to go out, they didn't care about the football schedule or the practice the next day, they just wanted to party when they wanted to go out.

Enjoying the night life and going out a lot led me to coming in contact with some people who were doing illegal activities and I got involved. I did it for the money. At the time, I didn't think I was doing anything real serious. But it turns out that they were counterfeiting money and that's why I went to jail and ended up in state prison.

I was not a violent person and I had never committed a violent crime. But I liked going out at night. I would have a drink from time to time, but I wasn't much of a drinker. I'd have a drink from time to time. But I was passing counterfeit bills to pay for things. I was not printing the money; it was being printed by other people. I was not involved like that, but I was using that counterfeit money to buy things.

I didn't realize it at the time, but I was being used by other people. I was being exploited. I didn't see it. I didn't see other options for making some money. They were using me to further their life and their goals, and I did not see it. People who looked at me might think I was mature because I had some size on me. But I was still just eighteen, nineteen years old. I was just a young kid who was naïve.

I got arrested

In 1976. I was arrested in my hometown in Alabama. I was arrested for possession of forged documents. I had been passing counterfeit money. I got convicted, but I was not sentenced to serve time in jail right away. The criminal justice system knew me from my high school days, and I had a good reputation. I was the kid who went to Tennessee State University on a football scholarship. So, instead of sending me immediately to jail, they wanted me to go back to college and then during the summer I would be in jail in Alabama. That was good for me. But I got discouraged. While everyone else went home from college, I spent several summer months in jail between my freshman and sophomore years, which sapped my enthusiasm and motivation. It was a tough time. But I persevered and I completed my sophomore year.

I came back to Florence. I got on the road and visited some people I knew. I got deeper into the night life. During this time, I was not happy, and I did not know what I was doing with my life, but I had a feeling that I did not want to go back to what I had been doing. So, when it was time for my junior year at Tennessee State, I did not go back and only completed two years out of my four-year scholarship. I was not focused when I went to college. It was definitely a missed opportunity in my life.

I got married

In 1980, I married my first wife, Debbie Cole Simpson. We met at a family cookout in the backyard of someone's home. We started seeing each other and things clicked between us, and we decided to get married. This marriage ended in divorce in 1998.

I got arrested and sentenced to prison

In 1983, I faced legal trouble again, getting arrested twice for passing counterfeit money. Despite being non-violent offenses, I became a habitual offender due to three similar charges. While the crimes were not severe, I was categorized as such, potentially facing a 60-year sentence. Fearing the Three-Strikes Law, I accepted a plea bargain for 20 years, unaware of my right to legal advice.

Facing imprisonment, I ended up at Kilby Prison, a classification center in Montgomery, Alabama. After a brief stay, I was transferred to Draper Prison in Elmore County for the next two decades. The shock of the transition from my previous life to prison was profound.

Assigned a 6-digit DLS number, now known as the AIS number, prison life became a stark reality. Memories of following strict security protocols, such as placing palms on the wall when someone passed, remain vivid. Today, the younger generation in Alabama prisons tends to disregard these traditional practices.

Reflecting on my time as an inmate, the quality of food remained consistently poor, a sentiment that seemingly persists today.

The Commissary

You need money to buy food at the commissary because prison food is just so bad. I had set up a commissary account which allowed people to donate money. When I first went to prison all we had was cash money. Today inmates have credit cards and stuff like that.

We would go sign for our money and have cash on us. They had a sandwich shop next to where we signed for our money and that's where you could go to get something that tasted decent.

One day I got my $20 bill and I turned to walk away, and two guys came up to me. They were going rob me of my $20.00. One of them had a shank (a little knife). When I realized they were about to rob me of my money, I jumped one of the guys. I took the knife from him and stabbed him, and the other guy ran away. Protecting my $20 dollars got me another 20-year sentence. They decided to run that 20-year sentence concurrently with my current sentence. They also decided that I needed to do some time in lock up (solitary confinement in a single cell).

I was in one lockup for about 8 months. I came out one hour a day to go into the yard and I stayed in this cell for 23 hours a day. I did not have any store privileges. I did not get any books. I got nothing.

If you want to break a man, put him in consolidated confinement. You are locked up in one cell. You don't know what time of day it is; you don't know whether it's night or day. You don't know if it's 7:00 in the evening or 7:00 in the morning.

It was crazy back then. There were a lot of murders in prison. We wore our own clothes; we didn't wear a prison uniform. We wore our own tennis shoes. We had cash money which means of course that people gambled anytime and anywhere. We could walk the yard. We did not have cell phones, so we used the public payphone.

When I go into prisons today, it seems completely upside down from when I was an inmate. Recently, I was in a prison that was named the Georgia Diagnostic Center. I was there with my son Josh, and it was his first time visiting the inside of a prison. I was in shock. I saw a prison staff person walking down the hall with a case of water on his shoulder and prisoners were walking by him. When I was in prison and a prison staff person was walking toward me, I had to stop, turn around, and put my hands on the wall until the staff person passed by.

Seeking God

When I went back into the population that was when I started seeking God in my life. I was looking to change my life.

My job was adult basic education, which for me was a pretty good job. I worked with a woman from Calhoun College and that was good. I was what they call a runner in prison. I worked for a lieutenant who had authority and I did errands for him and delivered things that had to get to others in the prison. I had good literacy skills, but there were many people in prison who did not have good reading skills. Most of them had not finished high school.

My sisters drove from Florence to visit me. My mom, who was my biggest cheerleader in my life, was not able to make the drive to the prison. But we stayed in contact. She had seen me in the best of times and in the worst of times and she knew my life would change.

Kairos Prison Ministry

I had been in lockup, and I was trying to adjust. I had started going to the chapel and I heard about Kairos, so I applied for a weekend Christian Kairos Ministry Retreat, and I was accepted. I didn't know what to expect, other than what the inmates were talking about. Six months after the retreat, I accepted Jesus into my life. After that, I faithfully attended the regular worship services and made a life commitment to God. I was called into the ministry. Participating in the Kairos Prison Ministry was a life-changing experience for me.

I vividly remember that Kairos Prison Ministry was an organized structure that did not have anything to do with denomination. Although it was a Christian ministry, it was just for everybody. Kairos is a very unique ministry. Even though we had different people from different denominations, it is all about God. It is all about Jesus. It was not about the denominations. People just come together, really show Christian love, being an example of what the church should look like. While we were incarcerated, everybody was the same. Some of those people were doctors, some of them were judges, district attorneys, and so forth.

When a person goes through a Kairos, their life will not be the same. I was lucky to participate in the Kairos Weekend Ministry Program while I was in prison. It was just one weekend, and it was very powerful. It really did something to me and changed my life and I believe the other 20 – 30 inmates were also changed.

In prison, you don't get much food, and they brought in all this food during that weekend. They always had cookies on the table, sandwiches, and good food. When we went back to the dormitory after the first day, we couldn't wait to go back the next day. Each day was a full day of learning and it really resonated with me. It was a special time.

I got saved in prison because that's where I got the word. Kairos Prison Ministry got me saved. I turned my life over to God. I started on the path of really studying the bible. I could quote all the scriptures, all the books in the Bible, the Old Testament, and the New Testament.

When I was in prison, I never dreamed that I would be coming back to prison to minister to people. But today, when I minister to people in prison or after they have been released, people light up with me. They know that I can identify with them because I was there, I was in prison, I lived it. After completing two years of being incarcerated, I was assigned to the Chapel to assist other inmates in the GED program.

A new release program for non-violent offenders

Six months after participating in the Kairos Prison Ministry's weekend program, I was granted release through the Supervised Intensive Restitution (SIR) Program in Alabama. Aimed at non-violent offenders, this community-oriented initiative allowed for an earlier return home than my original 20-year sentence.

Amid prison overcrowding, the SIR Program permitted me to serve my time while reporting to a parole officer weekly until I became eligible for parole. After making parole, my reporting frequency gradually decreased—from once a month to eventually once a year—completing the entire 20-year sentence through this process.

During my parole, I engaged in prison ministry and returned to the prison on Saturdays. This commitment spanned four years in prison and 16 years on parole.
Facing the transition to freedom, I grappled with "gate fever," a term encapsulating anxiety and anticipation before release. Despite knowing I would eventually leave, the challenges of maintaining vigilance in a prison environment filled with various offenders remained significant. Individuals experiencing gate fever, especially those confined for a decade or more, grapple with numerous questions about housing, meals, job training, family reunions, and employment.

Having gate fever meant constantly addressing these concerns while navigating a potentially risky environment. It's a challenging period where some individuals, eagerly awaiting their Monday release, might jeopardize their freedom by getting into trouble. This situation can be devastating for them and their peers who anticipated their departure.

After Prison

When I was released and got out of prison in 1987 I had so much peace. I was always praising God. It was a special time for me and God. I got into the word. I told God I was going to run my life for him. When things got rough, I just dug in and believed in God. God told me not to worry.

My wife Debbie and I were blessed by three wonderful children. In 1988, our daughter Britney was born; in 1989, daughter Latosha (Tasha) was born; and in 1990, our son Joshua was born. I named him Joshua because I was into the word.

New Life Church of God in Christ and Pastor Anderson

In 1990, I joined New Life Church of God in Christ in Florence, Alabama because that's the church my wife went to. This was a period in my life when I was mentored by Pastor Anderson, and I got started with reentry ministry.

The pastor was Elder Larry Anderson. It just so happened that we had grown up together. He was just a few years older than me. He had been good to me when I was in prison, writing me letters and sending me cards. I always appreciated that. After joining the church, I got under his wing. I was a young minister coming out of prison and I wanted to be obedient. I began going to state meetings, district meetings, and the national convocation. I came from the old school to the Church of God in Christ. I was very impressed by Elder Anderson's leadership in the church. He even had a relationship with the presiding bishop.

Our friendship from the earlier years in my life got me in the door with him. Back then, I was a real fireball. I still get fired up, but not quite as much as I was back then, some 30 years earlier than now.

I remember that when I went to Church of God in Christ meetings, they gave young ministers like me three minutes to speak. At first, I would get up and start talking and thank God for being here. I learned that when we got up and read scripture, it was to everyone in the meeting. It's like going down a runway because those three minutes speed right on by. While reading the scripture, we had to break it down and then with a whoop, we had to bring it on home. I quickly learned that when I stood up to read scripture, I was honoring the bishop. Because of my style, I had the feeling that I was a favorite in all of the meetings.

I wanted to become an elder in the church and I wanted to move up in the church. They sent me to All Saints Bible College in Memphis, Tennessee for my ordination. I began driving back and forth to Memphis. It was about 150 miles each way. Sometimes I stayed on the weekends. I did that for about 18 months. While attending All Saints University, I started Reentry Ministry and I later incorporated it as Outreach Reentry Ministry, Inc. on that special day of February 7th, 1991.

I was ordained an Elder

I was still in Florence, Alabama. After that time of study in Memphis, I went to the state's Holy Convocation (in Alabama), and I was ordained in the church. Jesus just called me in. During this period, I received several Ministerial Counseling and Community Service awards.

It was a special time. I had been ordained as an Elder in the Church of God in Christ, First Ecclesiastical Jurisdiction District in the State of Alabama. That was special. I was now a Licensed Minister. Now, I was able to put on the whole armor of God. It was special. I was ready and things began to change. I was getting invitations to speak as an ordained Elder to different churches.

Lacey Springs, Alabama

About a year after that, a church became available in Lacey Springs, Alabama, which is about 15 miles from Huntsville, Alabama and about 75 miles from Florence. I was asked by the Bishop and my Pastor, Larry Johnson, to go and oversee those people. I went there and I pastored the church for a little over a year. It was a small church with many elderly people. I did what I was supposed to do, the normal Sunday thing, Wednesday night Bible study, all of that. I had an office in the church and during the week I was able to work on my prison ministry. As time went on, I just decided that it wasn't for me. I told the Bishop, who had become a Superintendent, that I was going to step down from the church. I was with the Church of God in Christ for about five years.

Pastor Anderson

I want to pay a special respect to Pastor Anderson because he played an important role in my life. I learned so much from him and I use many of his lessons in my work today. I learned about leadership from Pastor Anderson.

He had a certain aggressiveness because he wanted to achieve things. He was moving up in the Church of God in Christ. He was a pastor. Then he became a Superintendent over several churches and then he became one of the bishops. I saw his aggressive drive to want to get ahead, to keep going forward, to get to the top. He did not stand still; he kept moving because he wanted to achieve things.

I admired that he was a strong leader and preacher. He was very good with administration and organizational matters. He had a special relationship with the parishioners. He was also a family man. To me, he was something special because he had all those skills and attributes. I would not be where I am today without the lessons, I learned from him. What can I say, he impressed the heck out of me.

But there was a "but" for me. He had that little thing about other churches, Baptist churches, and Methodist churches. I mean he grew up in the Church of God in Christ. All during this time with the Church of God in Christ, I was seeing something different than what I saw in the Kairos ministry. In the Kairos ministry, they accepted all the denominations, whereas the Church of God in Christ only accepted the Pentecostal Christian denomination.

Through my own self-discovery, I realized that it really mattered to me to be in an environment where people felt acceptance for whatever denomination they were from. What I had learned in my prison ministry was impacting me now.

Pastor Anderson was a lovable person. During the national holy convocation in Memphis with thousands of people, he was on stage with the national Bishop of the Church of God, and he had a heart attack right there. I will always remember that moment, just as I always remember Pastor Anderson and what I learned from him.

St. Mark Missionary Baptist Church

Later on, I began my work with St. Mark Missionary Baptist Church which was located in Florence, Alabama. At St. Mark Missionary Baptist Church, I was the associate pastor and first administrative assistant under Dr. Bishop Boyd. In the basement of the church, we had a full-time prison ministry and we helped offenders in prison, ex-offenders, their family members, and the homeless population.

Before setting up these services in the church, we were providing these services out of my house. I had developed the passion to help returning citizens with outreach services and transitional housing.

Although we were providing services in the church to returning citizens, things were not necessarily smooth and easy. We had the ministry for returning citizens in the basement. We had a situation in the church because we were doing something in the morning time.

Here is what happened.

The church's location is downtown, and the work release program was also downtown in the Salvation Army facility.

They would let the inmates out to find a job. They got out about 6 a.m. and If they did not find work, they were on their own till much later in the day. So, during the day, they would be downtown hanging around the park or the library. They did not have anything to do because they couldn't go back to the Salvation Army till six o'clock at night. Many of the people were homeless. Guys were just walking around. When it was cold, they would try to get in the library because it was warm inside. But basically, they had nowhere to go.

I looked at the situation, and I said, "Well, I'm going to open up the church in the morning time to help these people." I figured that we could help these people. Finding a job is hard. In many situations, people can't just show up and fill out an application. We had a few computers, and I thought the people could come to the church in the morning to fill out applications, get some coffee, and enjoy fellowship.

I started telling the guys to come over to the church in the morning time. Several people started coming over to the church. The word got out that you could go to the church for coffee, cookies, and fill out job applications.

Now, I had a flock of homeless people, and a flock of inmates, coming to the church.

Everything was cool with these people, they were well-behaved. But church secretaries and church ladies would come to the church. They started talking to Bishop Fisher about the situation because for them, it was a real problem. There was a conflict for them. They were coming into the church, and they were seeing homeless and returning citizens coming in and out.

The Bishop called me into his office, and he asks, "Do you think you can have these people out of the church before nine in the morning? The ladies are talking."

I said, "I can't do that" and I explained my thinking to him.

I told him that I can't put a time limit because this is what I do with the ministry. This is what the people needed because they could not go back to jail too early or back to the Salvation Army. They feel lonely. They can drink coffee here in the church and be on the computer. I listened and took it all in. I decided about confronting the ladies about this during Bible Study. Then I went up to the sanctuary to lead the Bible study.

I was sitting in the sanctuary and Bishop Fisher asked me to teach. I said, "No sir, you got it."

After the Bible study, I got up and the women were sitting together in the church. I say, "Mothers, can I ask y'all something for a minute?" They say, "How are you doing?" I say, "I'm doing fine." I said let me ask y'all something, "I'm hearing that y'all got a problem with the people that I'm dealing with who I bring into the church."

They said, "Yes, we got a problem with it." And we talked about it. They had problems with our helping the inmates and returning citizens. And I said, "Let me tell you something. Did you not know that Jesus was in prison when he was crucified?" I said, Jesus wasn't guilty, but he was an inmate. Jesus was an inmate."

The conversation finished up and I went back downstairs. I was very upset.

Arlinda

In 2000, I met Arlinda Brawley when she worked at the Muscle Shoals Electric Board. When I was paying our utility bill, I met her at the window and we kind of clicked. We went to lunch. I realized she was a strong person. We married in 2000. She became strong in the prison ministry and was 100% behind me. It was a blessing to me that my ex-wife Debbie and her became like sisters. Debbie and I had reconciled and that made a huge difference.

Arlinda got very involved in our ladies prison ministry. She was dedicated and she went with me into prisons, when I traveled, and went to meetings. She was great.

Hotel for Returning Citizens (People Released From Prison)

Around this time, Chester McKinney came to see me. He owned McKinney Lumber Company, which was a very large company. He needed employees. He was interested in our work release program because he needed employees. I explained the situation we were having at the church, and he told me that he had an old hotel next to the lumber company. I got very excited, I mean, he had a hotel.

We had about 80 people involved when Mr. McKinney came to see me about a program. He had an idea of using the work release program and using a bus to get the people to and from the work locations. He came to me with the hope that I could help him. Of course, helping him would be helping all the people we were helping, so it was a win-win situation.

Mr. McKinney says that he would like the hotel to be housing for the inmates and we want to donate it to you. We will give it to you. We will give you all the money that you make at the hotel, and we'll pay your salary and move all your stuff over to the hotel.

Bishop Boyd, Chester McKinney, and I drove over to the hotel, and we pulled up right in front. I said, God bless us with this. Bishop Boyd had not been in the meeting, so he wasn't fully tracking what was going on.

I said, "I had a vision and God gave this to us." Very soon after that, I moved the ministry into the hotel and that's how this program began to grow. We had 70 rooms. We got jobs for the people. We had the food. We had the training. We had the computers from the church. We had everything.

I felt so great to be able to serve the workforce. We got up to about 10 or 12 guys in the hotel, which was called Full Way Hotel. We were doing really good. Everybody was straight.

I got a call from a sheriff in South Alabama. He said, "Elder Simpson, I hear you run an outreach ministry up there." I said, yes, we do, it is called The Full Way Reentry Program. (Later on, we changed the name to The Full Way Outreach Ministry and Reentry Program.)

The sheriff was calling because he had a sex offender that needed help. I had been in prison ministry all these years, but I never did much study and research. If a person would call me and they had been in prison, then I would want to help them. I didn't care what the person's crime was … robbery, murder, or something else, I just wanted to help.

Yes, Sheriff. I have some room here. We can help. The person does not have to sleep on the courthouse steps.

He sent the registered sex offender to the county register as a sex offender with the probation officer. We provided housing. Everything was working as it's supposed to. Unfortunately, the sheriff had not sent out the notification letters in the community like he should have and that became a problem.

The word got out that we had violent sex offenders in our program. People in the community went to the city and county commissioners, the mayor, and the chief of police. The media would often swarm our location with cameras and microphones. They actually came to my home. They wanted to know if we had sex offenders in the hotel. Being in the local paper and the cameras and being on the local news went on for about a month. It painted me as a bad man.

We had countless meetings, with the county commissioners and the city council. It was the election year at the time. We had a meeting with the Attorney General. We had a meeting with everybody. Because our accountant had set up our organization as a faith-based organization, the government agencies couldn't shut us down because we had not violated the law.

Then, they sent the fire marshal to the hotel. He did an inspection, and everything was fine. He approved everything. We were doing the right things. Pressure was put on the fire marshal, and he came back for another inspection of the hotel. He said, "You all don't have any fire sprinkler systems. We have to shut this place down until you get sprinkler systems." This time he said that we needed fire extinguishers.

Then, Chester McKinney and the McKinney family came to me. We had about 12 people staying at the hotel, and we weren't going to put people out on the street.

The families had to go and find apartments and houses. It took us about a week to get all those people placed. After we got the people situated, I told Chester that we were going to shut down the hotel. That was difficult.

About a month later my wife Arlinda passed away.

On the night that she died, I was at a program. Arlinda had planned to go with me, but at the last minute she decided not to go. When I got home that night and went inside the house and went into the bedroom, I began talking to her. But she did not say anything. She had passed away.

I remember when my wife passed. Chester McKinney and his brother Joe came over to my house and told me they don't want me to worry about anything. They would pay for my wife's funeral, pay for everything. It's kind of private, that family is still behind us. We are 100% right with them today.

When I was in prison, I had an encounter with the Spirit of God. I had an interaction walking around the gate. And God showed me about being faithful, about opening doors and sending people from north, south, east, and west. That was 20 years earlier. When my wife passed, I had the same experience in that room.

After Arlinda passed, I was in a real bad place. I was at home and there were a couple of friends looking after me. It took a while, but after I got myself together, I said to myself that I'm not going to let these people back me into a corner. They thought they could stop me, so I turned my house into a transitional home. The outreach reentry's minister's house. I did it out of anger. I thought to myself: I own this house. I own this property. People can come onto my property if I let them. I lived in a nice neighborhood with a nice house. I am going to turn my house into a transitional home.

I met with a city official and a county commissioner. They agreed that this is my home and my property, and that people couldn't come on the property without my permission.

That's how we started. We've been doing transitional housing from this house since 2018. Then we got another house for women, a ladies facility. In 2023, we had about a 95% success rate as meaning returning citizens who completed the program. We keep about four or five guys in the house at all times. We still have a deal with the lumber company. We have about four or five different employees there. We can get a person who has been released from prison a job within 48 hours. The person does not have to be living in our facility.

We work in an area known as The Shoals which contains cities and towns such as Florence, Sheffield, Tuscumbia, Muscle Shoals. Other areas include Lauderdale County, Lexington, Rogersville, and Killen. We made a major impact in the area that we that we were in, in having friction with those state officials. I think that kind of got us branched out to where we need to be.

The sheriff was never against us. He just didn't issue the letter. Later, we got an apology for that. He knew it was his fault for all that happened because the hotel was on the line of the city and the county. The sheriff tried to put that stuff on the police chief. At a County Commissioners meeting, I remembered the sheriff was talking to the people in the audience.

There was a door in the back of the room and the police chief walked in. He just stood there. It was funny to me because the police chief just looked at the sheriff and rolled his eyes because he knew the sheriff was wrong. Everybody was against us but McKinney, the guy that gave us the hotel. He and his family are very successful businesspeople.

He and the McKenna family stood with us. They never turned their back on us. We are still doing work release and using buses today.

Mr. Chester McKinney is a hero to me.

I'm nothing special, but I was able to make the hotel work for transitional housing, until we needed to get the extra fire sprinkler system. I love what I do. I realize now that when I went to prison God saved my life. I went to prison in 1983 during the crack epidemic and God saved my life, he saved my life.

He showed me. I'm going to give you something you can't get at the University of Alabama. You can't go to Harvard to get it. We can't go to the library and get anything on this. You can't go to classes to learn this. Humm. Now we have people teaching this information. I really thank God for what God has given me. I really do. I didn't go to school to learn what I am doing now.

Prison Ministry becomes Outreach Reentry Ministry

When we started doing prison ministry nobody else was doing it. You had Chuck Colson, you had several people, but nobody was doing prison ministry like we're doing it back in the late 80s.

Back then, when you told a person you've been in jail you were looked down upon by others and yourself. We usually had desperation on our face. If you looked at someone the wrong way, someone might call the police on you. If you went to church to pray, you see women putting their pocketbook close to them because they are worried you might steal it. It was crazy. I hope to make it less crazy for people getting out of prison and reentering society.

I met Chuck Colson in the 1980s. I went to a conference that Chuck Colson had, and I met him. You may remember him as a former White House Counsel for President Nixon who later founded a Prison Fellowship.

At the time, our ministry was called Reentry Ministry. There was a man at the conference who also had a Reentry Ministry. So, we changed our named to Outreach Reentry Ministry. I was already doing outreach reentry ministry in Alabama. We had a three-phase program, with these three steps: preparation, transition, and stabilization. Our program was designed for ex-offenders and family members in the community. With our preparation phase, we were preparing men and women to get out of prison.

During our transition phase, the person went into a transitional home, and received counseling, skills training, and related assistance. Our stabilization phase was our long-term effort, and we collaborated with agencies, the ex-offender family, the community, and civic and social leaders. It's a long-term program.

We set it up like an AA program, because those of us that are returning citizens, because people need continuity of support to help them through their adjustment period. We all need support. Even for me, I need support. I've been out of prison for over 37 years, and I still get gate fever and I still need that support from people I can identify with.

Black Wall Street USA

In 2017, I met Mr. Mohammed. He was working with Black Wall Street USA, and he moved from Texas to Alabama. Black Wall Street USA was developing a farm program and they needed people to work in that program. They were trying to get black clients to work in the farming industry.

I told him that you got the wrong information about Alabama. I didn't know what somebody in Texas told you, but people who just got out of prison are not going to work on a farm. They need a different kind of job. They need a job where they have insurance and things like that.

Somebody told him about me because I was working with ex-offenders in our reentry ministry. He came to visit me to learn more about our stabilization aftercare program. He and the Black Wall Street USA people liked what we were doing. He had never seen a program like the one we had at the Father's House Church. It impressed him and he asked me if I have ever thought about joining Black Wall Street. Later, Mr. Mohammed moved from Texas to Alabama, and he took on the position of the Alabama State Director of Black Wall Street USA.

Mr. Muhammad would repeatedly ask me, "Do you want to become part of Black Wall Street?" Based on what I knew at the time, I was not interested. It was not on my radar. I was doing what I'm doing. I didn't see how it would tie into what we were doing at the time because Black Wall Street USA was dealing with economics and finances. I didn't make the connection on how Black Wall Street USA could tie into what we were doing.

He said to me, "I'm going to put you on my executive team in Alabama." He registered me in the Black Wall Street USA organization and paid the $65 yearly fee. I filled out the application and he sent it in. Then, he put me on a state committee, but I never went to any meetings or anything like that. He and I would talk on the phone, but I never went to any meetings.

Mr. Muhammad stayed close to me because Black Wall Street USA needed what we were doing with ex-offenders. When The Black Wall Street USA Executive Director Dr. Carter and others found out what we were doing with ex-offenders, it was amazing to them that we could run such a program … using our three-phase approach to bring inmates out of prison and getting them jobs or help them develop an individualized home plan which clarifies what services will be provided to the returning citizen.

One day, I got a telephone call from Dr. Michael Carter, Sr., Founder of Black Wall Street USA. He was in California with his executive team. I had never spoken with him before. He asked me what I thought about taking over Black Wall Street USA's Inmate Reentry and Recovery program.

I told him my wife had recently passed and it was not a good time to talk. We prayed together. I asked him why they called me. They told me they needed a leader. They were praying for somebody to take over their Inmate Reentry and Recovery national department, because the former Chicago-based national director left the program. They needed somebody to take that position. When they got through praying in their meeting, they saw that my paperwork was lying on the desk. They took it as a sign to give me a call.

I knew it was an honor to be speaking with Dr. Carter, but I did not want to deal with it at the time. I even hung up on him because I did not want to talk. However, Dr. Carter was persistent. He called me back a few months after that initial call, telling me again that he wanted me to lead the Black Wall Street USA's Inmate Reentry and Recovery program and take it nationwide.

At first, they just wanted a platform to get their message out. They didn't have a program. But I would be able to provide the substance of the program with our three-phase approach (preparation, transition, and stabilization), which I had been working on for years. They were a national program, and my operation was a very small organization. We had the experience and the credentials, and they needed us.

I decided to accept the position. It was huge for me. It was a confirmation about me, and all the work I had been doing after getting out of prison and on the path of helping ex-offenders (returning citizens). Now, I am about to lead a national organization's Inmate Reentry and Recovery program.

When people learn about Black Wall Street in Tulsa, Oklahoma, they read about the bombing, the economics of George Washington Carver, and that people were making a lot of money because of the oil rush out there in Greenwood. But there was one aspect nobody was dealing with. It was the people in jail for various crimes such as bootlegging. Nobody was talking about the dark side of Black Wall Street. Dr. Carter and his leadership team wanted us to tackle this dark side.

The national reputation of Black Wall Street USA was a platform. When people first came on with me, such as my vice national director, my administrator, and people like that, they thought there was a salary involved in that. But there was no salary. The national reputation of Black Wall Street USA was our platform for us to generate our own finances with this national platform.

With God, things just started happening. We met people and we expanded. I could see the work of God moving to help us and the ex-offenders. And we made so much progress by the grace of God. God did all that. I watched him put it together. I watched him help us through our ups and downs and he showed us that he was going to take us someplace we had never been.

This was in 2018.

When I began leading this program, I looked at it as an opportunity for me to reach a national audience, with my ideas and track record of getting results. I didn't take the position for money reasons. I didn't even ask them how much they were going to pay me. After I got on board as the National Director, we just started building and going forward. We established the National Redemption Project, a name that was coined by Dr. Carter. Expanding the National Redemption Project became my focus.

My first Vice National Director was Vernon Key. I remember that when I told him I wasn't getting paid, he was a bit in shock. I said, "Man, I ain't getting paid. God told me there is no job any better than this one. God told me to go out there and work and then you will be paid."

We just kept going. I was traveling quite a bit. I was meeting people in person. We were telephoning and having conference calls. Back then, we had a national telephone conference every month. It was every week on Thursday. In fact, we still have this weekly call. But back then, we would have the weekly call and very few people participated. Back then, it was mostly me, Dr. Carter, and maybe one or two other people. I was pretty darn sparse. But we believed it was important, so we kept at it every Thursday.

Then, all of a sudden, people started coming on that call from Chicago, New York, California, Alabama, Texas, Costa Rica, and other locations. It was amazing. That was in 2000. It was so gratifying to me. When I was back in prison 20 some years earlier, God had told me that he was would send people to me. I didn't know how he was going to send them. I didn't know how it was going to come to pass. Now it was happening.

I can't explain where all these people came from, but God sent them to us. It was just our time. We had people from all over the country, representing state agencies, nonprofit organizations, and churches. We talked about the National Redemption Project and issues we had with the criminal justice system.

It's just another example of God moving to help us.

As the National Director of Black Wall Street USA Inmate Reentry & Recovery my assignment was to work with our 60 Member National Committee to assist community Agencies, Ministries & Organizations across the country and in Central America through our National Redemption Project as we assisted the returning citizens and the homeless through our Twenty Steps to Reentry & our Threefold Vision.

We partnered with the Salvation Army nationally in 2020 thru 2021 during the Pandemic We offered on Substance Abuse Classes, Stabilization Aftercare, GED, Entrepreneurship, Workforce Development, Job Placement, Computer Literacy and Money Management classes are offered by Auburn University.

Thank You God

It all came from that vision I had from God when I was in prison. It was like a spirit spoke to me and said, "I'm going to send people to you. Take this ministry to a whole other level."

When I was in prison, God had showed me a vision. He showed me a vision when I got saved, I was walking around the yard. And I asked God. I said, God, give me something to do. I was told to be effective in helping people. And God just showed me. It's like many spirits that look up in the sky. I'll give you as far as you can see, all you have got to do is stay with me.

God started sending people. I met Brunetta and met these people that I'm dealing with now. I'm in Atlanta right now. I didn't know these people. God sent the people. I didn't send a resume out. I didn't send a flyer. I didn't do an advertisement, any of that stuff. From that day to this day, man, I can't tell you where all these people have come from. People have gotten saved. Husband and wife have gotten back together. I have strong relationships with judges, district attorneys, mayors, Congressmen, Senators.

It's God. God promised me when I was in prison. He was gonna put all this stuff together. And everything you see in my life now is God. I ain't got no explanation for it. I can't write it. I can't go to the library and get a book on it.

Everything you see God putting it together. I can remember doing this program, I didn't have a dime, didn't have a good hourly job to pay my bills, none of that stuff. I didn't know what money was coming in. But I kept moving. I just kept moving. God opened doors and it's been amazing.

In 1991, I founded Outreach Reentry Ministry, Inc., a 501[c]3 organization. That's what we were doing when Black Wall Street contacted us. We took that over with Dr. Carter, Black Wall Street USA. We established a national redemption project out of that program.

There really came a transformation in my life, my life completely changed. Changed, changed in industry in this way I would change the things that manifested themselves in my life right now. Like when you start talking about leadership, I really had a real revelation from God and God showed me if I just walked with him, you know he would do the rest, and somebody say if you take one step got to take two. I have to disagree with that because I feel if you take one step you gotta go all the way.

See you can cry all you want to cry. You can preach all you want to preach. You can testify all you want to testify that don't move God faith. You have got to believe you can do it. If you believe you can do it now you can step out on faith.

In 2021, October, I stopped my affiliation with Black Wall Street USA.

Outreach Reentry Ministry, Inc.

We designed a class for the Alabama State Prison System. It's a 9-week program one hour a week and the classes are out in one hour, so we do that. It is our preparation class.

Preparation, Transition, and then Stabilization.

First step is preparation so that class we teach in prison we teach you with the pre-release program preparing the man that come out of prison and by me having been an ex-offender going into prison we sent out applications throughout the prison Limestone and it's over 000 inmates at that present prison, so everyone wants to come down with class. The classes are popping into the prisons because of the way we teach; we create a dynamic class and people learn how to think.

We also collaborate with a lot of other organizations they deal with such as Auburn University for other classes, gaining credit for skills developed in prison, and job placement.

How do you get your driver's license? What will you need when you get out of prison?

Just prepping people, and those kinds of things do you recommend people in prison to go through the Kairos program absolutely. The Kairos program is a life changer. It's a game changer.

Re-Introduction

People in prison get released and they keep coming back to jail. Our passion at Outreach Reentry Ministry is to change this.

When I was in prison, I asked God to give me something. He did. He blessed me with this particular program that we're doing now through Outreach Reentry Ministry. What I am doing today goes all the way back to when I was in prison.

When I first started doing prison ministry nobody was doing it and no one wanted to hear about it. There were some people doing prison ministry in other states. I went to churches thinking that I would find a positive reception. But no. I knocked on door after door after door to talk about prison ministry but found little interest. I discovered that people did not want to talk about it. People were shutting their door on me. I was told that they would call the police on me if I did not leave. Even when I was only asking for minimum support, people did not want to talk to me. With a few exceptions, most people just shut their door in my face. I am happy to say that no one slammed the door on me, although there were times, I felt like they had.

I was in prison about 30 years ago. My prison identification number was 4-digits. There were about 300,000 people incarcerated in the United States. Now that number is 2.2 million. To say the prison system has grown since I was in prison, well, that's a major understatement. If I went to prison today, my prison ID would be 6 or 7 digits.

We are dedicated to eradicating mass incarceration, and we need your help.

Outreach Reentry Ministry, Inc. is a nonprofit 501[c] (3) organization dedicated to providing Transitional Aftercare Programs throughout the United States and Central America. Currently, we are serving adult and youth men and women in Alabama, Georgia, Mississippi, Michigan, Ohio, Missouri, Illinois, and Central America. Our programs provide support to those applicants for the development and implementation of comprehensive and collaborative reentry strategies specially designed to increase public safety by reducing recidivism.

Our vision is to provide services to prisoners, ex-offenders, and their family members. We provide aftercare support for the development and implementation of comprehensive and collaborative reentry strategies specifically designed to increase public safety by reducing recidivism!

As one of our outreach reentry volunteers has said:

> "We are always excited to see the inmate get out
> and succeed. **It ain't over** is one of the sayings
> here at Outreach Reentry Ministry and
> it's a slogan that seems to keep everybody going.
> After all, if God is for us who can be against us!!!!!!!!"

This chapter highlights our work and passion at Outreach Reentry Ministry to help returning citizens, to help society, and to help reduce mass incarceration.

Helping with Higher Paying Jobs

We have been fortunate to help people who come out of prison to get a higher paying job and sometimes career jobs. We help people plug into employment opportunities where they get career jobs. We accomplish this because we have built relationships with corporations. Whenever possible, we connect people to $30 and $40 an hour opportunities. Sometimes that is not the case, and people get a fast food or entry level job. But our goal through training and coaching is to help the person develop skills so they can earn more money.

Our life skills classes and mentoring also helps the person become a productive citizen who goes on to get their own place, their own care, and get back to a good family life. Whenever possible, we want to be life-changing when we help people.

Our Seven Spiritual Principles

We are guided by these seven principles:

(1) The Spirit of the Lord
(2) The Spirit of Wisdom
(3) The Spirit of Understanding
(4) The Spirit of Counsel
(5) The Spirit of Might
(6) The Spirit of Knowledge
(7) The Spirit of Fear & Reverence of God

We deal with offenders and ex-offenders, regardless of color, race, and creed. If you are an ex-offender, it doesn't make any difference about your skin color, ethnicity, or religion. I know that organizations collect data on whether you are black, brown, or white. Are you Asian, African American, Latino, or Caucasian. We don't care about all that. We are concentrated on helping the individual.

We stay in our lane. If you are an ex-offender, we can help. If you are in jail or prison, we can help. If we get a call from a homeless person, we refer them to an organization that works in that area. When we get calls about people who sell, buy, and abuse drugs and alcohol, we refer them to a drug and alcohol center because that is not our specialty. Of course, when we stay in our lane, we are always on the lookout for collaborative opportunities to help people and communities, where organizations with different specialties work on a common goal.

We don't try to do everything. Our goal is to do one thing well.

We got a call just yesterday about an ex-offender who recently went blind. We discovered that he does not have any knowledge about medication. We discovered that he had experience in putting a transmission in a car. A blind many who put a motor in a car blind! You have to admit that seems pretty wonderful. He met all the requirements in our program, so we were happy to admit him. Right from the start, he was getting along with the other guys.

Over the years, we have grown in our experience and abilities. We deal with a myriad of situations. In one situation, we had a person come into the program who was a paranoid schizophrenic. He was released from prison and came into our program. We found out that he was getting medication while he was in prison. He seemed okay. But after a while something was not right, and we did not know what was wrong with him. We finally took him to the emergency room. Then, we took him to a mental health center. That's when we found out what was wrong with him. He was a paranoid schizophrenic.

Sometimes we work with people who have a blood sugar problem. We spoke to family members and got him to the hospital. He had diabetes but did not know that.

We have dealt with a whole lot of issues.

Success Rate

We had a 95% success rate with our program. Approximately 95% of the returning citizens in our program completed it.

We manage and operate **The National Redemption Project** and therefore are active and involved with the following programs and activities:

- Classes and Forums
- Transitional Aftercare Programs (for men and women)
- Criminal Justice Reform and Stopping Mass Incarceration
- Partnering with State Government and Higher Education
- VOTE YOUR VOICE CAMPAIGN (in Partnership with Southern Poverty Law Center's Voter Rights Restoration Project)
- Youth Diversionary Programs for At Risk and High-Risk Youth
- Celebrating Women
- National Entrepreneurship and Job Placement
- CDL (Commercial Driver's License) Logistics Program
- Project Angel Tree (for children)
- Formerly Incarcerated Convicted People and Families Movement (FICPFM)

Let's review some of these.

The National Redemption Project (Three Step Approach)

We strive to meet the needs of returning citizens and we focus on needs in these areas:

- Social
- Intellectual
- Spiritual
- Emotional
- Environmental
- Physical.

To accomplish our goals, we use a very effective approach that includes three steps (phases). It is directly focused on helping ex-offenders and their families and the homeless population.

This chart describes our three-step approach.

STEP ONE PREPARATION	Beginning 6 to 12 months prior to release, volunteers focus on equipping the prisoner with skills, education, and resources needed to make a successful transition to the outside world.
STEP TWO TRANSITION	When the ex-prisoner leaves the prison gates, reentry volunteers make sure he or she has safe housing, food, clothing, and many other key supports. During the early days of release, most ex-prisoners need daily encouragement and assistance until their initial crisis-level needs are resolved. Then they need continued weekly contact, spiritual guidance, and emotional support for 6 to 12 months as they find employment, begin to rebuild relationships, and adapt to their new life. We offer outreach Aftercare Transitional Housing.
STEP THREE STABILIZATION	Volunteers continue to coach and assist the ex-prisoner toward establishing consistent

| | personal habits, healthy relationships, spiritual growth, and a church commitment.

One very important sign of stabilization is when the ex-prisoner becomes involved in serving others in the community instead of expecting to be served.

This phase is an ongoing process which consist of individual counseling sessions and bi-weekly group sessions.

Successful reentry ministry involves addressing the needs in all areas of the returning citizen's life: social, intellectual, spiritual, emotional, environmental, and physical. It is also possible for a person to be stable in one area of life, but barely surviving in another. |
|---|---|

Classes

We offer daily and weekly classes with a strong curriculum covering many essential topics, such as:

A. Substance Abuse AA / NA / Celebrate Recovery
B. Trauma / Gate Fever Education
C. Root Based Therapeutics / Mental Health
D. Northwest Shoals Community College / Ready-To-Work Classes
E. Auburn University / Financial Literacy
F. Stabilization Aftercare classes for Ex-Offenders & Family Members
G. Workforce Development / Entrepreneurship
H. Job Placement / Maintaining Employment
I. Computer Literacy
J. Transitional Housing
K. Assist with obtaining Identification Cards / Social Security Cards
L. Assist with obtaining Snap Benefits
M. Nutrition
N. Credit Report Adjustment
O. Civil & Social Rights Responsibilities
P. Voting Rights Restoration
Q. Homeless Assistance
R. Southern Poverty Law Center / Vote Your Voice Campaign
S. CDL (Commercial Driver's License) logistics Program
T. Southern Center for Human Rights
U. The Innocence Project
V. At-Risk and High- Risk Youth Diversion Programs

W. The Vote Your Voice Campaign

Forums

We offer a Weekly Open Forum, and we are involved with the Georgia Criminal Justice Forum.

Transitional Aftercare Programs and Facilities

My vision is to have transitional programs and facilities in different states.

The Outreach Transitional House of Alabama offers transitional housing to men reentering society after incarceration. Our programs provide support to those applicants for the development and implementation of comprehensive and collaborative reentry strategies specifically designed to increase public safety by reducing recidivism.

I just feel that now is an important time. It seems that everybody tells us that they have been directly affected by the criminal justice system, or they know someone who has been affected.

In past years, it seems that the field of corrections and people leaving prisons were someone else's concern or domain. Historically, that would be former inmates, people working in corrections and parole, and government officials and staff. It would also include church leaders and teenagers.

In today's world, we have a greater awareness that so many things are interconnected and here are a few examples:

- Human resources managers who need to hire.
- Returning citizens who are making a life transition and are likely to go back to prison if they do not get appropriate services.
- Community colleges that want to be relevant to populations of people who might have been neglected in the past.
- Church leaders who want to do more.
- Literacy programs that want to play a role to help youth and adults succeed in life.

Yes, our vision is to have transitional programs and facilities in different states.

Criminal Justice Reform / National Entrepreneurship and Job Placement

Now I want to share a few things about our Criminal Justice Reform / National Entrepreneurship and Job Placement missing, vision, and goals.

Mission
Bridge the gap of unemployment to financial security and make a difference by providing high quality content and services through education that empowers the community.

Vision
Have locations in every community where people can come and create new opportunities using our curriculum.

Goal:
Help individuals through our strategy and action plans that consist of:

- Analyzing their learning skills
- Designing a way to address the knowledge and skill gap
- Developing materials and lessons plans
- Implementing the plans in the classroom
- Evaluating our success to ensure that it works
- We want our students to become long-term working citizens in our community

Partnering with State Government and Higher Education

We partner with the Alabama Extension Services & Auburn University to offer educational assistance to our clients. This includes:

- Test Prep Services
- Work Keys Testing
- Ready to Work Classes
- Digital Literacy Classes
- High School Diploma Options for our Students
- Money Smart Classes
- At Risk & High-Risk Youth Programs

VOTE YOUR VOICE CAMPAIGN (in Partnership with Southern Poverty Law Center's Voter Rights Restoration Project)

Outreach Reentry Ministry partners with the Southern Poverty Law Center (SPLC) in Alabama to work directly with returning citizens to encourage democratic participation, support individuals in the process of registering to vote, and in exercising their right to vote. Through our The National Redemption Project's **VOTE YOUR VOICE CAMPAIGN**, we collaborate with SPLC's **Voter Rights Restoration Project** in Alabama.

There are 2.3 million disenfranchised voters across the five states of Alabama, Florida, Georgia, Louisiana, and Mississippi. These individuals cannot weigh in on issues of importance to their lives because of policies and processes that prohibit or hamper their election participation. Outreach Reentry Ministry's The National Redemption Project has been part of the conversation on the definition of the Alabama Moral Turpitude Act (HB 282) of 2017 which finally clarified which felonies, state or federal, will not disqualify Alabamians from voting. This is part of the process of restoring the right to vote to tens of thousands of people in Alabama.

Project Angel Tree (for Children)

We have assisted thousands of children of those that are incarcerated through our: Annual Project Angel Tree Program which is held on the 19th of December. In some years we have assisted over10,000 children with Christmas gifts and a special dinner.

We started the Angel Tree Project a long time ago. We needed a fundraiser to generate some funding for the organization. We looked around at different approaches such as the Salvation Army ringing the bell in front of stores to raise money. We decided to piggyback on what Chuck Colson was doing in his ministry with the Angel Tree Project. At the time, nobody was wrapping gifts at the mall. We decided to do an Angel Tree program with a tree in the mall. We contacted the mall and found out they liked the idea because it was so worthy, and no one was doing it. Back then, none of the stores were wrapping presents.

The mall donated us a spot. We went to local people we knew who owned or worked at businesses. We asked for help, and we got tape, paper rolls, and boxes. Most of the boxes were very large, so we went to JC Penney's, Sears and other stores and they donated smaller boxes. Nobody knew how this fund raiser and wrapping gifts project was going to go. But we believed in it, and we tried. It was very successful. We set it up in the mall and people were coming through the mall, giving donations, and having their gifts wrapped. In that first year, we were trying to raise $10,000, but the final number was much, much higher than that.

We also went to the city and county jails and put gift applications inside the chapels. When the guys came to the chapel, they would fill out the applications for gift for their children. We would get the applications and follow through to get gifts for the children. When the children came up to the tree in the mall, we made angel decorations for them which they would put on the tree. The children also got gifts. Here's a fun fact. In our first year, the kids got sometimes 2, 3, or 4 gifts because we had more donations than kids.

It was so successful that we took the idea to the counties near us, and we asked pastors to do something similar for children in their area. We asked pastors and churches to sponsor kids and some sponsored 10 Kids and some sponsored 25 kids. We got all these gifts coming in from churches. We set up our programs the Thursday or Friday before Christmas. We would go to churches with a tree and with gifts to go under the tree.

With just four or five volunteers, we did that for about five years. It really helped to instill the meaning of Christmas. In later years, the program morphed into setting up wrapping booths at Walmart and Kmart. Customers were happy with the service, and it was a very good fund raiser for us. I even became a professional gift wrapper because I had initial training and coaching, plus an hour of practice. Do you need to know how to wrap a package, so it is beautiful and make a bow out of the tape? Just ask me how. The angel tree and the gift wrapping brought a lot of joy to everyone who participated and of course it benefited the children. People want to help. We just need to ask them and give them a path.

My sisters came out to help and we had great help from senior citizens, teenagers, people from churches, and many others. Everyone wanted to make those wrapped presents look beautiful. It was a lot of fun and very meaningful.

And the donations came in. Sometimes one or two dollars and sometimes ten or fifteen dollars. I encourage you to brainstorm on ways to raise funds and help people. Perhaps you will have a Project Angel Tree for homeless or unemployed people.

We're touching hearts and minds and making sure that people feel appreciated.

Formerly Incarcerated Convicted People and Families Movement (FICPFM)

We are aligned with FICPFM, which is a national movement of directly impacted people speaking in their own voices about the need to end mass incarceration, America's current racial and economic caste system. To that extent, FICPFM is committed to transforming society by transforming the criminal legal system.

Here is information about their mission and vision:

Mission

The Formerly Incarcerated, Convicted People and Families Movement (FICPFM) is a national network of civil and human rights organizations led by people with conviction histories and their family members. Committed to transforming society by transforming the criminal legal system, we advocate legislatively, judicially, through direct organizing and stakeholder education in the communities where we live and serve.

Vision

We envision a world where we do not use punishment and prisons as answers to economic, political, and social problems. We are striving to develop a world that produces healthy outcomes for everyone impacted by the criminal punishment system and abroad.

I Challenge You

In this chapter, I want to describe several challenges I have for you.

This chapter is organized into these areas:

- Youth
- Church
- Government

My Challenge to Youth

I challenge you to put on the whole armor of God so that might be able to stand against the wiles of the devil. There is a battle between the spiritual and the physical. I tell you; we get too much into flesh. I remind you to keep your mind right. If you can get your mind right, you can get anything right. Keep your mind together. The devil wants to get you off your game and other people want to get you off your game. The devil wants to get to your mind and other people want to get to your mind.

When you stay on your game and when you can keep your mind right, things will work out for you. Please remember that dealing in the spiritual world is armor against future demonic spirits. A lot of the time we fight against something we can't see. And because of that, we need to remember that it is a mind thing, and we must keep our mind right.

What does it mean to put on the full armor of God?

The amazing period of my life is when I went to prison. While in prison I found God in my life because I was so low every day. I never thought about suicide, and I never thought about killing myself. Stuff like that never came to my mind. When the court handed me my 20-year prison sentence, I thought my life was over. But I found God, and I learned about putting on the full armor of God.

I want you to know that putting on the full armor of God is important to all youth. Where are you today in your life? Are you a youngster under the age of ten? Are you a teenager in school? Are you already working for wages? Are you in college? I ask that you please put on the full armor of God to protect you.

Are you engaged in the political process so that your voice is heard? Are you involved in voting rights? Are you involved in choosing candidates to represent you at the local, state, or federal level? Okay then, learn about putting on the full armor of God.

Does leadership interest you? If you feel you can lead others, then you will want to be the change that you want to see in your community, your state, our country, and our world. If you are not a resident of the United States, what leadership do you want to bring to the country you are in?

I want you to remember that leadership is a true gift from God. You are either a leader or you are not a leader. As a leader, please put on the full armor of God to protect you.

When you put on the full armor of God, you can use that to propel you to your goals. With the full armor of God, you can push back against the devil and adversity. With the full armor of God, you will be able to see light even in the darkest hours. Sometimes you can be down so low that all you have is God.

I charge you to put on the whole armor of God.

If you are going to a destination, consider that you might or might not be going in the correct direction that gets you to your destination. You need to assess your path or direction. If you are on the correct path, that is good. If you are not on the correct path, you need to be courageous and strong to change your direction. It's like being on a road and you realize you are not going in the correct direction. Okay, you need to make a change and that kind of change is good for you. Sometimes, you need to turn completely around to get going in the correct direction.

You need to put on the whole armor of God, and you need to be willing to turning around if you are going in the wrong direction. Because we know that we will never reach our destination if we are going in the wrong direction.

If you're 16 or 17, or any age, and if you are having difficulty, then take some time and find out why you are having the difficulty. If the difficulty is that you are going in the wrong direction, you need to be courageous to try to turn your life around.

My Challenge to the Church

I challenge you to be like Jesus. Whether we are dealing with inmates, inmate families, or people who have been released from prison, we need to be like Jesus.

I ask that you remember that prison life and incarceration impacts people from all walks of life. When we think about the people we see in our neighborhoods, in the grocery store, in a doctor's waiting room, driving on the highway, riding a bus or subway, it is likely that prison has touched some of these lives. We need to remember that almost everyone has been affected by the criminal justice system in some way.

I believe that we all need to do more to help people who leave prison to not go back. I believe that we must be careful how we treat people, and we must be conscious of the work that we are supposed to be doing. We need to remember and practice the words from Matthew 25: Jesus shows us that true faith doesn't stay locked within the walls of a church building. It reaches out to people who are hurting and facing injustice — and it cares for children, who are the most vulnerable of all.

We need to remember that Paul, who you read about in the apostles, was incarcerated. And of course, we all remember that Jesus was in jail because he was falsely accused.

It is my belief that churches need to develop more bridges to people who are returning citizens. It is my belief that churches need to do more work to help these people.

I believe that we need to recognize the progress that we have made, and we need to make much more progress in helping returning citizens. I remember a time when churches were not receptive to me and my message, but today we have much more reception. Let's recognize our progress and do even more. We can preach to returning citizens and everyone is more receptive, and we can present the message of Christ. More people realize that they may know someone whose son or daughter is in jail which means people are receptive.

I believe that some church leaders and members are in denial about the needs of returning citizens and it is my hope that churches increase their role in helping returning citizens become positive forces for themselves, their employers, their communities, and for God. I have written this because people were not receptive initially.

I believe we can accomplish a great deal.

As church leaders and congregation members, we need to do that work that God commissioned us to do. Faith is looking at something being in the spiritual world before it manifests itself in the natural world. This means that most of our struggle, our fight, is in the spiritual world dealing with the devil, dealing with demons, and spiritual wickedness and things that we can't see.

As a returning citizen myself, I now understand. I see God opening doors that wouldn't necessarily have been open. I feel so excited that I've gone through the prison experience. I really do because it has produced growth in me.

I know my life has changed. I had that encounter with God. I want more and more returning citizens to have that encounter with God and I ask that churches work hard to make that happen. I was determined to just do the right thing. I want to do the right thing, say the right thing.

Do unto others as I would have people do unto me.
I wanted to be like that. I wanted to follow the golden rule.

My Challenge to Government

I ask that you increase your efforts at helping returning citizens become responsible citizens and productive members of society.

We must do more to give people a second chance.

Our three-phase approach of Preparation, Transition, and Stabilization has been successful, and we need your help to keep improving it and to expand it so that it reaches more people. We need to increase collaboration within our communities and throughout each state. This will help us stretch our resources (time, money, and effort) to help returning citizens. With collaboration we can also be more innovative. The payoff is enormous.

We must work together to reduce recidivism which will reduce the cost of government services in this area. We must work together to help make people (returning citizens) whole, so they have pride and their families and children become whole and have pride.

We must work together to upskill people for today's jobs and future jobs. We need to have returned citizens become income producers. I ask that you invite our organization to the table when you are brainstorming on solutions to employment, job training, homelessness, housing, transitional services, and related.

www.ingramcontent.com/pod-product-compliance
Lightning Source LLC
Chambersburg PA
CBHW032102020426
42335CB00011B/451